IMAGES
of America

CHELMSFORD

WORLD WAR I MONUMENT ON THE NORTH COMMON VINAL SQUARE. This was dedicated in honor of Alberton W. Vinal, who died in the war.*

IMAGES
of America

CHELMSFORD

Chelmsford Historical Society and Garrison House Association

ARCADIA
PUBLISHING

Published by Arcadia Publishing
Charleston, South Carolina

Library of Congress Catalog Card Number: 2008943450

For all general information contact Arcadia Publishing at:
Telephone 843-853-2070
Fax 843-853-0044
E-mail sales@arcadiapublishing.com
For customer service and orders:
Toll-Free 1-888-313-2665

Visit us on the Internet at www.arcadiapublishing.com

CENTRAL SQUARE IN THE 1890s. This photograph was taken looking west toward Wilson's Hotel, Sweetser's Market, a horse trough, and the hay scales.

Cover Image: WHITTEMORE'S CARRIAGE MANUFACTURING AND PAINT SHOP. The shop was located 1 mile from the Center on North Road. Pictured here are, from left to right, Arthur E. Reed, Charles Cole, Floyer J. Whittemore, unidentified, Thomas Sheehan, and unidentified.

CONTENTS

ACKNOWLEDGMENTS

We would like to thank the many people, groups, and businesses who assisted us in gathering information and photographs: the Chelmsford Copy and Secretarial Center for word processing the original script, George Merrill, Gloria Hines, Mary Partridge, and Debbie Taverna for pictures, L. Charlton Greene Jr. for correct dates, Eugene Dziczek, Donald Pattershall, Richard O. Sr. and Mary Lahue for final proofreading, and Eleanor Parkhurst for her many suggestions and expertise on local history.

CHELMSFORD SIGN ON THE CENTER COMMON.

INTRODUCTION

The history of Chelmsford is a rich tapestry of people, places, and events. We have attempted to illustrate a small part of this wonderful heritage. *Chelmsford* has been produced through the collaborated effort of two organizations that have been established to protect and preserve artifacts from the past. We recognize the need to educate the public, especially schoolchildren, in the importance of their roots in the community. We have selected pictures from our archives and personal collections, reflecting the changes that have occurred over the past 340 years.

In 1652, a group of individuals from Woburn and Concord requested permission from the General Court to explore land west of the Concord River. The General Court granted permission to the individuals on the condition that they provide as much tillable land for the Native Americans as they had around their former planting ground near Robin's Hill and that at least 20 families move to the area within two years. Chelmsford was incorporated as a plantation in 1655 and the original boundaries were determined. Northward, Chelmsford ranged up near the Merrimack River, to what is now Lowell. Southward, it reached the Pawtucket Canal. To the east, it was bordered by the Native American land Pawtucket (known as Wamesit after 1686). Chelmsford reached southward down to the Patuxet Stake on the Concord River, which is now the Chelmsford-Billerica line. Southwesterly, the Native American land Tadmuck or Zadmuck (now Westford) created the border. To the northwest, the land was unoccupied. In 1656, the territory was expanded north to the Merrimack River and west to the Groton line. In the 1700s, parts of Chelmsford were annexed to Littleton, Westford, Billerica, Carlisle, and Lowell.

Residents held the first town meeting in 1654, at the home of William Fletcher on Crosby Lane. The earliest land allotted was for a town common and a site for a meetinghouse. The General Court had ruled in 1635 that no dwelling should be built more than one-half mile from the meetinghouse. This was to ensure closeness for safety from Native Americans, as well as to assist one another and work together as a unit. Early homes in Chelmsford were usually cottage style with one or two rooms downstairs and a loft upstairs. Families were large and lived almost entirely upon farm products made at home.

The population continued to increase as people came to work in the mills, and new families established homesteads. The increased population demanded increased services, schools, and housing. Libraries were organized in the 1700s "to improve the minds and morals of men laudable and praiseworthy." Classes were held in homes until the first school was built around 1718. By 1800, there were 12 district schools. Early social life consisted of corn huskings, training militia, ordinations, house raisings, sleighing, and dancing. Transportation was mainly by horse and wagon until the Middlesex Canal was built in 1804, and the railroads arrived shortly thereafter. Industries were started to meet the needs of the people. Natural resources were utilized for power and material. Skilled workers, including a tailor, a blacksmith, a weaver, and a miller, were able to contribute to these needs. The first meetinghouses were formed by religious groups that had previously traveled elsewhere to church. Many began their services in the town hall or Odd Fellows Hall before benevolent people donated land.

Chelmsford, at the crossroads of Routes 3, 4, 27, 40, 110, 129, and 495, has continued to grow and meet the needs of its people. Today (1998) Chelmsford (22.8 square miles) has a population of 30, 175. Within its boundaries are various industries in several industrial parks, restaurants, conservation land, recreational facilities both privately and publicly owed, nine school buildings, 20 plus houses of worship, nursing homes, an Alzheimer's unit, assisted living facilities, a retirement residence, elderly housing, apartments, condominiums, an "over-age-55" community, a mobile park, and public transportation.

Members of the committee were:
Nancy Clark
Nancy Dziczek, chairperson
Dianne Govoni
Mary Guaraldi
Mary Partridge
Donald Pattershall
Madeleine Pattershall
Debbie Taverna
Rebecca Warren
Editor
Eleanor Parkhurst

One

LANDMARKS

GEORGE H. WILSON BLOCK, CENTRAL SQUARE, CHELMSFORD CENTER, 1884. This large building was used as a hotel for a number of years. It is now converted into apartments with businesses on the lower level.

BARRETT-BYAM HOMESTEAD, 40 BYAM ROAD, CHELMSFORD CENTER, 1663. James Parker built the house and conveyed the property to Thomas Barrett. The Barrett and Byam families each lived there for over 100 years. Originally a saltbox house, it has been added on to many times. The homestead became the home of the Chelmsford Historical Society in 1968, through the generosity of Mr. and Mrs. Albert C. Murray. The homestead, Watts-Stevens Educational Center, and a Country Store are furnished with Chelmsford artifacts and are open for tours.

Garrison House — 1692   South Chelmsford, Mass.

THE "OLD CHELMSFORD" GARRISON HOUSE, GARRISON ROAD, SOUTH CHELMSFORD, 1692.
Home of the "Old Chelmsford" Garrison House Association since 1959, the house was one
of 19 garrisons in Chelmsford. Lt. Thomas Adams was the original owner, followed by the
Heywood family and the McCormick family from whom Warren C. Lahue purchased it. Lahue
donated it to the Association in 1959. The house was designated a National Historic Place in
1973. Many educational programs are offered to the public and second graders in the Chelmsford
schools throughout the year.

TOWN HALL, 1A NORTH ROAD, CHELMSFORD CENTER. Once the home of the town offices, including the police department, the building has been refurbished and is now utilized as a community center.

WORLD WAR II VETERANS MEMORIAL IN FRONT OF TOWN HALL, NORTH ROAD, CHELMSFORD CENTER, C. 1940S.

THE CHELMSFORD CENTER COMMON AND CHELMSFORD SCHOOL FOR THE DEAF. The School for the Deaf was the first in the nation to teach lip-reading. It later moved to Northampton and became the Clarke School for the Deaf.

REVOLUTIONARY WAR MONUMENT, CHELMSFORD CENTER COMMON, 1859. The Chelmsford Monument Association erected this monument to honor the men who served in the war.

MINUTEMAN BOULDER, CENTRAL SQUARE, 1899. Erected by the Molly Varnum Chapter, DAR of Lowell, this stone marks the spot where the Chelmsford Minutemen answered the call to arms on April 19, 1775.

PLANTING OF THE PURPLE BEECH TREE BY CHELMSFORD HIGH SCHOOL STUDENTS, CENTER COMMON, ARBOR DAY, 1891. From left to right are as follows: (front row) Sarah Redmond, Mary Bartlett, Ednah Byam, Christina Ashworth, Mildred Jefts, Alice Stearns, Harry Dutton, William Fulton, John Pratt, Arthur Harmon, David Perham, George Blood, Carl Mansfield, and Arthur Dutton; (back row) Lillian Santamour, Florence Cummings, Ida Melvin, Cara Hutchinson, Jessie Holt, Grace Chapin, Ethel Byfield, H. Gertrude Fulton, Grace Mansfield, Stella Byam, Ralph W. Emerson, Moses Wilson, Edwin Stearns, Charles Soderberg, Daniel Haley, Thomas Kearns, and Lyman Byam.

COL. SAMSON STODDARD HOUSE, CHELMSFORD CENTER COMMON. Now the site of the Central Baptist Church, the Chelmsford Classical School can be seen on the right.

VIEW OF CHELMSFORD CENTER FROM ROBIN'S HILL, C. 1924.

LONE PINE TREE, ROBIN'S HILL. The Lone Pine Tree was a landmark seen for many miles. Sailors could see it when entering Boston Harbor. The tree was cut down in 1885 during a ceremony in which a flagpole was erected in its place.

The famous BUTTONWOOD TREE from which this CITGO Station takes its name is Appox. 275 years Old, considered the LARGEST and OLDEST In MASS. On this SITE was built the HOUSE known as the 'ARK' in 1700 . . . .

BUTTONWOOD TREE, CORNER OF ACTON ROAD, CHELMSFORD CENTER, PICTURED IN 1971. Approximately 275 years old, the tree was in front of the 1770 house built by Dr. Nehemiah Abbott, known familiarly as "The Ark." The house and tree were razed to accommodate a gas station.

OLD MILL HOUSE, CENTRAL SQUARE, CHELMSFORD CENTER, C. 1678.

CENTRAL SQUARE, CHELMSFORD CENTER, C. 1950S.

MIDDLESEX CANAL TOLL HOUSE, CHELMSFORD CENTER COMMON, 1803. The Toll House was originally located in Middlesex Village at the entrance to the canal, now on Chelmsford Center Common.

FIRE TOWERS, ROBIN HILL, CHELMSFORD CENTER, 1939. A forest fire observer manned the towers, which were the highest points in town.

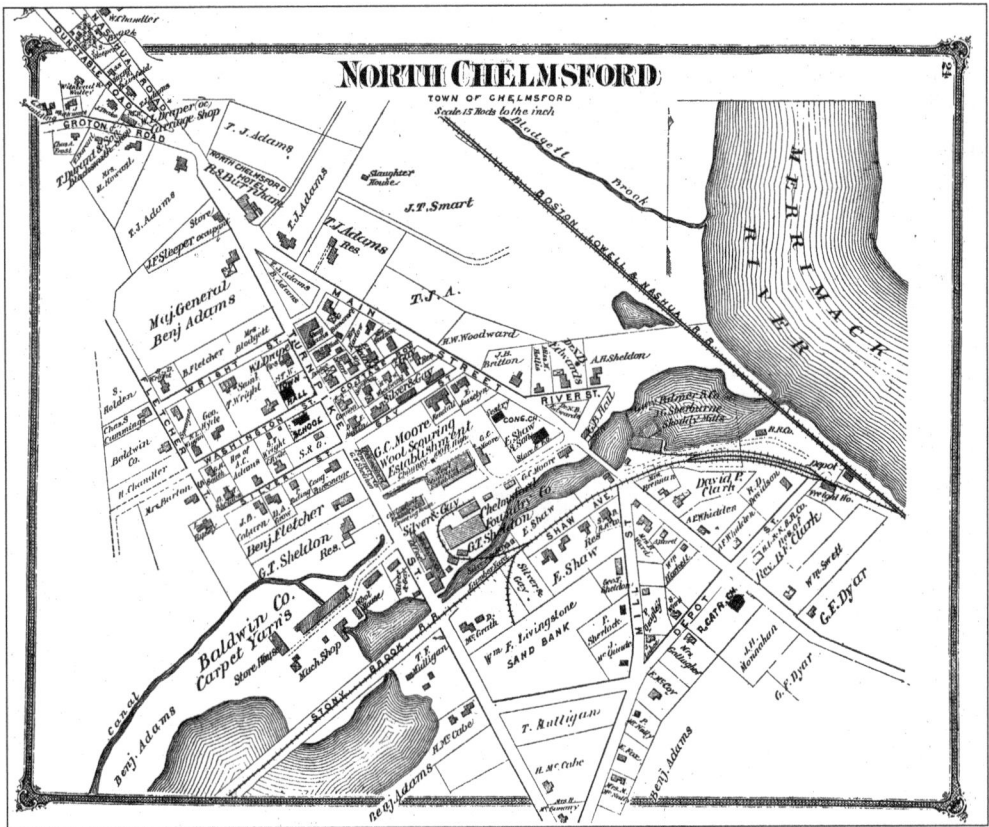

A Detailed Map of North Chelmsford with the Names of Residents on each Street.

Stevens Corner, Vinal Square, North Chelmsford. Trolley tracks ran through Vinal Square in 1912.

MAP OF NORTH CHELMSFORD, 1895.

LOOKING TOWARD CHELMSFORD STREET FROM 18 EVERGREEN STREET, WESTLANDS, APRIL 18, 1925. The homes belonged to, from left to right, Fred Carll, Bill Carll, and George Brown. Boyes' Barn and Store (later Henderson's Store) is second from the right, and the home at the far right belonged to Henrick Johnson.

20

Two

TRANSPORTATION

CHELMSFORD GINGER ALE TRUCK FLEET, LITTLETON ROAD, CHELMSFORD CENTER.

GENUINE BACKSEAT DRIVER, 1911. Mr. and Mrs. Wilfred W. Greene and family proudly display their car. The automobile was manufactured by the Watertown Auto Company three years before the Stanley Steamer.

HAROLD THE PACER. Shown from left to right are Clara Upham Whittemore, Susan Whittemore Wellwood, and Susan Whittemore Wellwood, who was Floyer Whittemore's sister (holding the reins). The horse, Harold, was owned by Floyer J. Whittemore and was never beaten in a race.

VINAL SQUARE, NORTH CHELMSFORD, C. 1930.

POLICEMAN DIRECTS TRAFFIC, CHELMSFORD CENTER, C. 1980S.

CHELMSFORD FIRE DEPARTMENT PUMP #1.

CHELMSFORD FIRE DEPARTMENT TRUCK, C. 1920s. Chelmsford Center Square Garage is now a mini-mall.

Trolley Car on Middlesex Street, North Chelmsford, c. 1930.

BOSTON & LOWELL RAILROAD (B&LRR) TRAIN. Nashua and Lowell Railroad (N&LRR) was chartered in 1836 and constructed 9.5 miles of track from Lowell to the New Hampshire state line to meet with the N&LRR. In 1880, this company was leased by the B&LRR for 99 years.

FREIGHT TRAIN, NORTH CHELMSFORD.

BOSTON AND MAINE RAILROAD STATION, MIDDLESEX STREET, NORTH CHELMSFORD.

BOSTON AND MAIN RAILROAD STATION, MIDDLESEX STREET, NORTH CHELMSFORD. This photograph was taken during the flood of 1936.

RAILROAD CROSSING, CHELMSFORD CENTER.

CHELMSFORD CENTER RAILROAD DEPOT, LITTLETON ROAD. A gas station is now on the site.

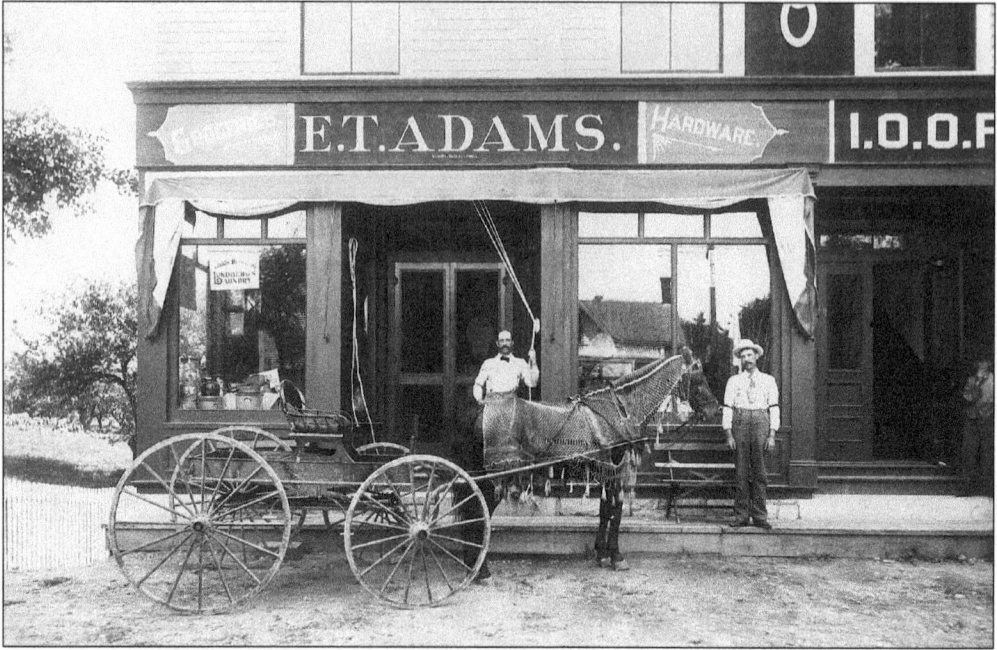

E.T. Adams Grocery Store, Odd Fellows Building, Central Square. On the left is Eben T. Adams, proprietor. Herbert Knowlton, clerk, stands to the right.

Harry L. Parkhurst Coal Sheds near Railroad Tracks, Chelmsford Center.

DUTTON BROTHERS (LATER SWEETSER AND DAY) GRIST- AND SAWMILL, CUSHING PLACE, CHELMSFORD CENTER. Shown here are, from left to right, Nels Nelson, ? Staples, and Clarence Nickles, who later owned an ice truck.

THE FIRST BUCKBOARD BUILT WITH A TOP, BY FLOYER J. WHITTEMORE. Taken c. 1880s at Willowdale, Tyngsboro, this photograph shows Mr. Whittemore at the reins. This buckboard was used to take people to the Robin's Hill Summit House for ice cream socials.

FOURTH OF JULY PARADE MARSHAL, 1923. Daniel E. Haley was the first elected president of the original Chelmsford Lions Club and a member of the Chelmsford Board of Registrars of Voters.

SPAULDING/REED HOUSE, 243 WESTFORD STREET, C. 1700. This house was built on land owned by Edward Spaulding, one of the early settlers. It is now the home of Leo and Theresa Patenaude. This 1872 photo shows the family of the day.

BAND CONCERT ON CHELMSFORD CENTER COMMON, 1905.

S.W. PARKHURST'S STORE. In this photograph the store is seen at its original location, before it was moved to the corner of Chelmsford Street. The original site is now occupied by the town hall/community center.

S.W. PARKHURST'S STORE, 2 CHELMSFORD STREET, CHELMSFORD CENTER. The move was made necessary by the coming of railroad tracks. This site was once that of a tavern. Henry Eriksen's Grocery Store was here for many years, and the building is now Dennis McHugh's Law Office.

Three

ORGANIZATIONS

NOVEM CLUB. An informal young men's social group of the late 1890s borrowed their sisters' and mothers' clothes for their appearance in the Fourth of July parade. The club took its name from the fact that it was organized in November. Shown here are, from left to right, Ralph W. Emerson, Arthur Cotton, William Hall, G. Thomas Parkhurst, Hawthorne Howard, Winthrop Parkhurst, Carl Ripley, Harold Davis, Will Fulton, and George Sturtevant (with banner).

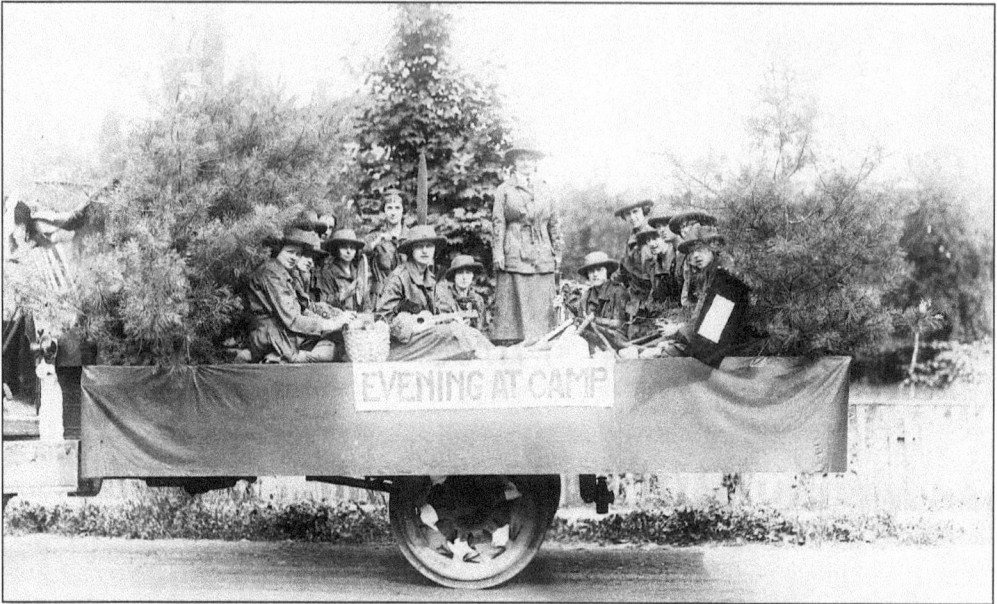

GIRL SCOUT FLOAT, "EVENING AT CAMP." Mrs. Charles Wells, leader, is standing. Troop I members, from left to right, are as follows: (front) Elsie Petrie, Barbara Parkhurst, Marjorie Scoboria, Mildred Silk, and Florence Ellis; (back) unidentified, Dorothy Davis, and Gertrude Jewett; (on rear of truck, at right) Esther Perham, Alice Wilson, Julia Warren, Thelma Shattuck, Madeline Lupien, and Margaret Robbins. Troop I Chelmsford Girl Scouts was organized in 1917–18 by members of Miss Esther Dane's Sunday school class of the Unitarian Church.

MEMBERS OF THE COMMANDRY, A MASONIC GROUP OF AREA MEN, AND THEIR LADIES.

Fourth of July Parade Float, 1923. The "coming scouts" are members of a brownie troop.

World War I Red Cross Ladies. From left to right are as follows: (first row) Ethel Wright and Nellie ?; (second row) Chairman Emma Perham, Adelaide Wright, and Pearl Adams; (third row) Mrs. J. Adams Bartlett, Miss Celia Richardson, Mrs. Julia Hall, Mrs. Nora Baldwin, Ida Paasche, and Emma Bartlett Dutton; (fourth row) Mrs. Walter Putney, Marjorie Coulter, Lottie Adams, Martha Warren, Louise Howard, Anna Searles, and Arimenta Paasche.

37

GROUP OF MEMBERS OF THE LOCAL ODD FELLOWS LODGE, C. 1907. From left to right are, Warren Cotton, George Parkhurst, Charles Nichols, Eben Adams, Warren Sweetser, Nathaniel Glidden, and Walter Winning.

Fourth of July Parade Float Advertising E.T. Adam's Grocery Store, 1907.

FOURTH OF JULY PARADE FLOATS, 1923, CHELMSFORD CENTER.

CAST OF ALL-AMERICAN ALBUM, 1940. From left to right are as follows: (front row) Mrs. Donald Fogg, Mrs. Edwin Warren, Miss Marguerite Hoar, Miss Marjorie Russell, and Constance Dane; (back row) Mrs. Lewis Johnson, Robert Clough, Mrs. Charles Dane, Roger Lapham, Mrs. George Hood, Miss Ruth Jefts, Mrs. Fred Laton, and Lester Ball.

FOURTH OF JULY PARADE FLOAT, 1923. Sidney Perham is on the bicycle.

COMMITTEE FOR THE TOWN'S 250TH ANNIVERSARY, MAY 1905. From left to right are as follows: (front row) Arthur Sheldon, Henry Perham, and George Snow; (back row) J. Adams Bartlett, Daniel Byam, Harry Parkhurst, Hubert Bearce, Joseph Warren, and Erastus Bartlett.

BALLOON AT LOWELL FAIRGROUNDS, GORHAM STREET, EAST CHELMSFORD, c. 1900.

OFFICERS OF THE INTERNATIONAL ORDER OF ODD FELLOWS LODGE, c. 1907. From left to right are as follows: (first row) Eben Adams, Howard Sweetser, Walter Winning, Charles Nichols, Warren Cotton, and Frank Worthen; (second row) John Scoboria, Isaac Knight, Almon Holt, Walter Emerson, and Russell Smith; (third row) Riley Davis, Mr. Rounds, George Wright, and Arthur Scoboria; (fourth row) Albert Perham.

FOURTH OF JULY PARADE FLOAT, 1923.

YOUNG MEN'S ATHLETIC ASSOCIATION (YMAA) SECOND TEAM, 1901. From left to right are as follows: (front row) Lawrence Marshall, Ben Cole, and Warren Blaisdell; (back row) Victor Parkhurst and Ralph Adams.

FOURTH OF JULY PARADE FLOAT, 1907. Shown here are, from left to right, Mrs. Fred Park, Mrs. Minot Bean, Ethel Bliss, Rachel Marshall, Julia Atherton, Mrs. Walter Bullock, Abbie Ford, Ethel Wright, Mrs. Pliney Bliss, Mrs. George Wright, Mrs. William Hall, Mabel Hatch, Mrs. Wilbur Lapham, and Mrs. Frank Spaulding.

HORNBEAM HILL GOLF COURSE TOURNAMENT GROUP. From left to right are as follows: (sitting) Frank Emerson, unidentified, Hawthorne Howard, and Charles Nichols; (second row) Harriet Emerson, Gertrude Fulton, unidentified, Mabel Fenderson, Percy Redman, unidentified, and Arthur Emerson; (third row) Edith Hagerman; (standing) Arthur Wright, Ed Redman, and Jessie Holt Wiggin.

FOURTH OF JULY PARADE WAGONS, 1907.

THE POST 212 AMERICAN LEGION DRUM AND BUGLE CORPS IN FRONT OF RAILROAD STATION, NORTH CHELMSFORD, 1936.

FOURTH OF JULY PARADE, C. 1970. The driver of the town hearse is Arnold Wilder of Westford.

CHARTER MEMBERS, FROM 1905 TO 1930, OF THE CHELMSFORD GRANGE. From left to right are as follows: (sitting) Herbert Sweetser, Nellie Hazen, Arnold Perham, Abbie Ford, and Fred Russell; (standing) Mrs. Frank Spaulding, Fred Fletcher, Frank Spaulding, Mrs. Eben Adams, Mrs. Fred Russell, and Francis Dutton.

46

Four

INDUSTRIES

LIME QUARRY, LITTLETON ROAD, 1736. Limestone deposits of excellent quality were about 2 miles long. Five kilns were operated by the Fletchers and Perhams. The last kiln, operated by David Perham, was closed in 1832. Caves and ruins of the kilns may still be seen at the site, which is now a Conservation area.

HARVESTING ICE, RUSSELL'S MILL POND OFF MILL ROAD, CHELMSFORD CENTER.

CONSTRUCTION OF ICE CHUTE, RUSSELL'S POND, CHELMSFORD CENTER. Arthur Warren stands to the top and left. Others in the photograph are unidentified.

Carpenter's Carriage and Blacksmith Shop, North Chelmsford.

MARINEL AND WILLSTEED STONE WORKS, NORTH CHELMSFORD.

SILESIA WORSTED MILLS, PRINCETON STREET, NORTH CHELMSFORD. This was the largest mill in town. It was sold to the United States Worsted Company in 1912 for $3 million.

EAGLE MILL, WEST CHELMSFORD.

SUGDEN PRESS BAGGING COMPANY, EAGLE MILL POND, WEST CHELMSFORD. The company was at the site of the Old Eagle Mill. The Abbott Worsted Company incorporated it in 1914. Cloth made here was used to make aniline dyes and press cocoa beans. The Hershey Chocolate Company bought pads to strain the chocolate. In the background is the William C. Edwards Farm barn.

Old Mill House Tea Room, 7 Acto. Rd., Chelmsford, Mass. Tel. 2-0597.

THE "ARK" HOUSE, OLD MILL HOUSE TEA ROOM, 7 ACTON ROAD, 1700. Ruby Emery was the proprietor of this popular tea room. It was razed and replaced by a gas station.

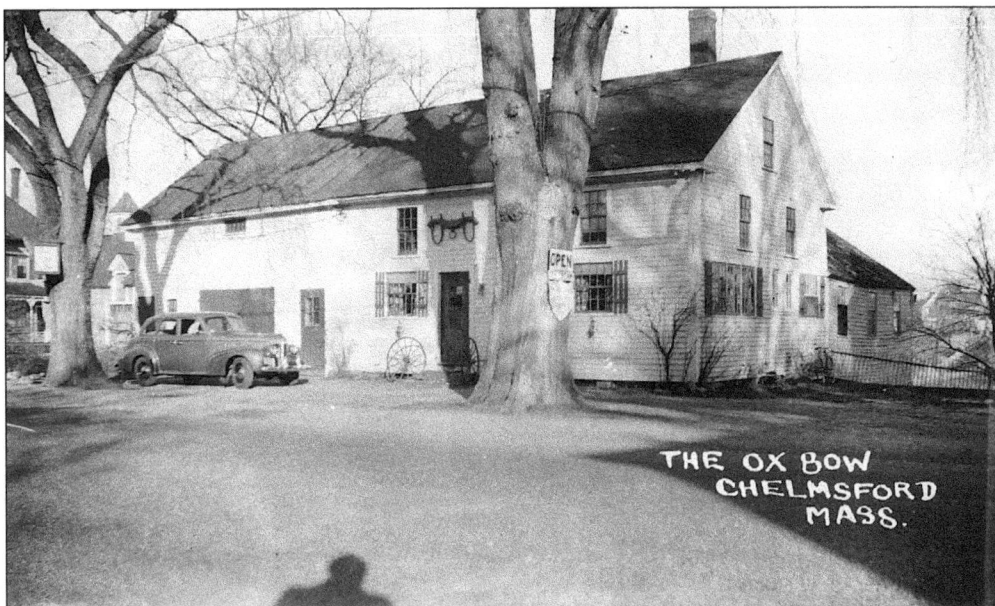

OX BOW TEA ROOM, 70 BOSTON ROAD, CHELMSFORD CENTER, C. 1950. Mr. and Mrs. LaForest Field were the proprietors of the tea room, which was formerly the home of Mr. and Mrs. Will Hall. The building was razed and replaced by the Carriage House Apartments.

THE INTERIOR OF THE OX BOW TEA ROOM, C. 1950.

EBEN R. MARSHALL'S BLACKSMITH AND CABINET SHOP. The barn faced South Street, now called Boston Road. American Legion Post 212 now owns the building, which faces Warren Avenue, Chelmsford Center.

SUMMIT HOUSE, ROBIN'S HILL, CHELMSFORD CENTER. The restaurant stood on the summit until it was destroyed by fire. It was a popular place to go for ice cream and other refreshments, as well as splendid views of Mt. Monadnock, Wachusett, and other mountains.

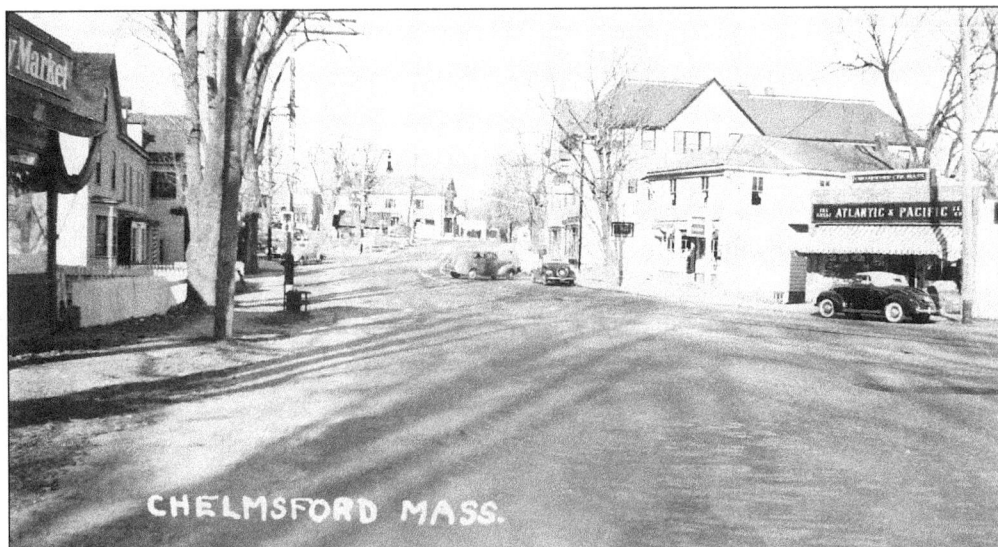

CHELMSFORD CENTER, C. 1940s. The Atlantic and Pacific Store on the right is now a medical building. The Page's Drug Store building is now occupied by an upholstery store. The independent market on the left is a coin shop today.

CHELMSFORD GARAGE, CHELMSFORD CENTER, C. 1910. Purity Supreme Super Market opened its first store at this site, after WW II.

250TH ANNIVERSARY, 1905. This U.S. Post Office building was owned by J.P. Emerson. R.W. Emerson was the postmaster. In 1930, the First National Store was located here.

SWEETSER BLOCK, 12 CHELMSFORD STREET, C. 1940s. The U.S. Post Office is located on the left and Hadley's Market is on the right.

SKIP'S RESTAURANT, 116 CHELMSFORD STREET, 1947. Built by the Kydd family, the Burliss/Gefteas family has operated the restaurant for two generations.

HENRY S. PERHAM HOMESTEAD AND CIDER MILL, WESTFORD STREET. Route 495 was constructed through this site in the early 1960s, and the buildings were burned for this purpose.

BYAM BLACKSMITH SHOP, 4 MAPLE ROAD, SOUTH CHELMSFORD, C. 1832. This land was purchased by Marcus D. Byam with the provision that a blacksmith shop be built and operating within three years. It was later operated by Daniel P. Byam. The blacksmith shop was moved to the Garrison House property in October 1977, the gift of Eleanor Parkhurst.

CHELMSFORD FOUNDRY COMPANY, NORTH CHELMSFORD, 1823. Originally set up by William Adams, General Leach bought it in 1824, filled in the breach, and re-flooded Newfield Pond, which became Leach's Pond, then Crystal Lake, and now Freeman Lake. The foundry operated until 1908 under varied management. (Courtesy of George Merrill.)

58

OLD GRIST MILL AT MILL POND, CUSHING PLACE, CHELMSFORD CENTER. The mill was once owned by David Perham, and later by H.C. Sweetser and George W. Day, and then the Cushing Grain Company. A sawmill stood so close it was almost adjoining. This was the site of the Captain Parker Mill, built in 1676.

JAMES AND SUSAN HILDRETH (VARNUM) WHITTEMORE, C. 1880S.

ADVERTISEMENT FOR THE **F.J. WHITTEMORE CARRIAGE MANUFACTORY.** As automobiles came into use and needed repainting, the smaller cars were painted upstairs and the larger cars on the ground floor.

HOME OF JAMES AND SUSAN WHITTEMORE, NORTH CHELMSFORD. Shown here are, from left to right, Emma Spaulding, Susan Whittemore, and C. Howard Whittemore. C. Howard was the son of James's and Floyer's brother.

GINGER BEER BOTTLE, CHELMSFORD SPRING COMPANY. A display of Chelmsford Ginger Ale artifacts can be seen at the Barrett-Byam Homestead.

COURTYARD OF CHELMSFORD GINGER ALE COMPANY, LITTLETON ROAD, CHELMSFORD CENTER, OCTOBER 1937.

CHELMSFORD GINGER ALE COMPANY, LITTLETON ROAD, CHELMSFORD CENTER. The Byfield Manufacturing Company was previously located on this site.

GENERAL STORE AND POST OFFICE, ACTON ROAD, SOUTH CHELMSFORD. Henry Emerson was the proprietor *c.* 1890s.

SOUTH CHELMSFORD U.S. POST OFFICE AND HORSE SHEDS, 321 ACTON ROAD, SOUTH CHELMSFORD. The store was built by Emile Paignon and occupied by storekeepers including Thomas Gerrish, Frank Bickford, Henry Emerson, and Charles Simpson. It is now called Kate's Corner.

PAIGNON GRAIN COMPANY NEAR SOUTH CHELMSFORD RAILROAD STATION. Agway is now located here.

64

NORTH CHELMSFORD MACHINE AND SUPPLY COMPANY, AUGUST 1924. The last men to work here were, from left to right, Lee Sawyer, John McAdams, Thomas Hill, John Daley, George Trubey, E. Davis, ? Dangerfield, Mike Ward, Norman ?, and T.R. Davis.

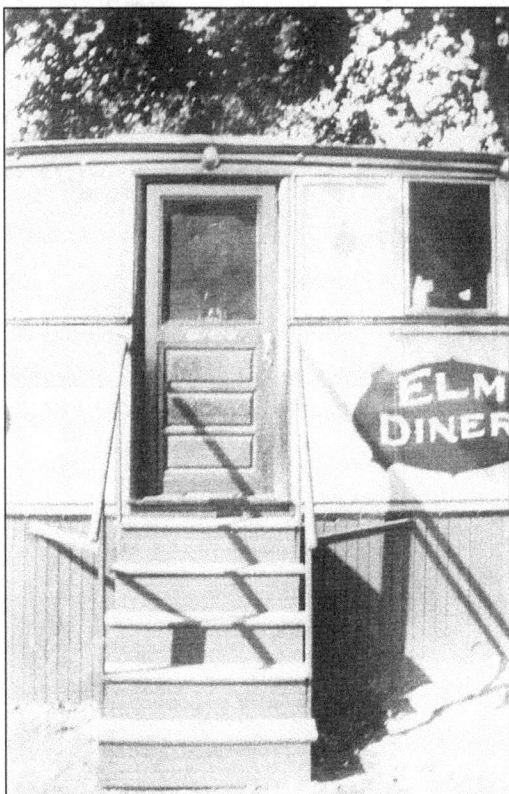

ELM DINER AT MILL ENTRANCE, 71 PRINCETON STREET, NORTH CHELMSFORD. The diner was a popular spot for mill workers and the general public. Joe Donovan was the proprietor. (Courtesy of Gloria Hines, daughter of Joe Donovan.)

65

GAGNON'S ROADSIDE STAND, 112 NORTH ROAD, C. 1950.

Five

HOMES

TYPICAL PARLOR OF THE 1800S.

CHRISTOPHER ROBY HOUSE, 203 MAIN STREET, WEST CHELMSFORD, 1831. Deacon Farwell is thought to be the original owner. He erected a factory for the manufacture of scythes. West Chelmsford became known as Farwell or Scythe Factory Village. The business was later purchased by Sawyer and Roby, who manufactured swords and sabers during the Civil War. Christopher Roby occupied the house at that time.

ROW HOUSE, GAY STREET, NORTH CHELMSFORD. This scene is an example of housing built by mill owners for their workers.

HOWARD HOUSE, 6 GROTON ROAD, NORTH CHELMSFORD, MID-1700S. This is one of the oldest buildings in North Chelmsford. It was part of the old Adams house Hotel in the 1700s and was later moved to its present site. Henry Howard, a carpenter, lived here in the 1920s.

POST OFFICE AND RESIDENCE, MAIN STREET, WEST CHELMSFORD.

ADAMS/PICKEN HOUSE, 14 MIDDLESEX STREET, NORTH CHELMSFORD, C. 1709. This house is pictured on a map dated 1709. It was originally a one-and-a-half-story house but, when the mill purchased it, the roof was raised and it became two-and-one-half stories high. The Wotton house is on the left.

CARRIE TYLER HOME, WRIGHT AND MIDDLESEX STREETS, NORTH CHELMSFORD.

SWEET/SHELDON HOUSE, 1846. George Gray built this house in 1846 for Charles Sweet. The house was built with a large rock left in the cellar. This 1884 photo shows Ada Maria, Clementine Anna, and Sarah Alice Sheldon.

MARSHALL HOUSE, 61 CARLISLE STREET, EAST CHELMSFORD, C. 1753. This was a famous tavern and stagecoach stop on the road to Boston. Thomas Marshall made his home here, and the house remained in the family until 1860. Thomas was the brother of Dr. Jonas Marshall, who resided at the Barrett-Byam Homestead on Byam Road at the time of the Revolutionary War.

FROST/CARLTON/DYER HOUSE, 114 GORHAM STREET, EAST CHELMSFORD, PRIOR TO 1753. This Frost family residence was a stagecoach stop and tavern. Thomas Marshall married Hannah Frost here on February 22, 1753. Early deeds indicate the Frost family also owned the brickyard on Brick Kiln Road.

EDMANDS HOUSE, 22 MARSHALL STREET, EAST CHELMSFORD, 1756. The original owners, the Edmands brothers, developed the first sugar beet. The farm was sold to the Marshall brothers in 1856, later sold to the Heaney family, and, in 1922, the Sears family.

MANNING HOUSE, 9 MANNING ROAD, EAST CHELMSFORD, 1752. This was the home of William Manning, inventor of the original corn-cake square made with ground corn and molasses, which he made on the premises. He became wealthy because of this invention. The house was a rest home for many years.

ROBERT PIERCE HOUSE, 21 MANNING ROAD, EAST CHELMSFORD, 1753. At one time, this was one of the largest dairy farms in town.

WINTHROP A. PARKHURST HOUSE, 9 ACTON ROAD, CHELMSFORD CENTER, 1901. This home was razed in 1973 in order to construct a bowling alley on the site. It is now an office building.

WRIGHT HOUSE, 200 ACTON ROAD, CHELMSFORD CENTER, C. 1842. This home was built about 1842 by Benjamin Chamberlain, the grandfather of Mrs. Lester Ball (Adelaide Wright). It was known as the Alcorn Farm for many years until the acreage was sold for housing.

DUPEE HOUSE, 246 ACTON ROAD, SOUTH CHELMSFORD, C. 1850. The house was built by Eli Parker about 1850; it is the second house to stand on this site. Jones Farm Stand is presently located there.

LYMAN BYAM HOUSE, 305 ACTON ROAD, SOUTH CHELMSFORD, C. 1830. Ezekiel Byam, owner of the factory that manufactured the first Lucifer matches in this country, was perhaps an early owner of the house. His descendants remained in the house until 1965. It was originally an one-and-a-half-story cottage. At one time a cobbler lived and worked here.

BARRETT/WRIGHT/PARK HOUSE, 12 PARK PLACE, SOUTH CHELMSFORD, PRIOR TO 1831. Joel Barrett Wright lived here in 1856, when the estate was purchased by Benjamin Clogston. In 1873, the Park family purchased the estate, and it has remained in the family since. Mrs. Charlotte Park DeWolf, first woman town clerk of Chelmsford, presently lives here.

HEYWOOD HOUSE, GARRISON ROAD, SOUTH CHELMSFORD. Miss Emmeline Heywood, one of the Heywood sisters, and her friend are pictured here in her garden. Some boards in the house are 34- to 36-inch-wide pine. The great central chimney rises from the center of the house. Garrison Road is at the extreme left.

76

BATEMAN HOUSE, 4 PROCTOR ROAD, SOUTH CHELMSFORD, 1779. John Bateman built this brick-end house. His daughter Charlotte married Ezekiel Byam, the match manufacturer, in 1818. Following their marriage, they moved into the house, and Mr. Bateman moved to Concord. For many years it was known as the Waite Farm and is now the residence of Mr. and Mrs. Charles Parlee.

BATEMAN HOUSE, 4 PROCTOR ROAD, 1779. The house was refurbished by Charles Parlee.

PENNIMAN HOUSE, 118 ROBIN HILL ROAD, SOUTH CHELMSFORD. Shown here are, from left to right, granddaughter Minnie Bell Brown and grandma Penniman.

MARCUS D. BYAM HOUSE, 11 MAPLE ROAD, SOUTH CHELMSFORD, c. 1825. This house was constructed in 1832 and raised from a one-and-a-half to a two-story house at the end of the Civil War.

DADMUN HOUSE, 6 BOSTON ROAD, CHELMSFORD CENTER. This view is as the house looks today as a medical office building.

CHAMBERLAIN/DUTTON HOUSE, 143 PINE HILL ROAD, CHELMSFORD CENTER. Samuel Chamberlain built an earlier house on the site; the present house was constructed about 1760 by Jacob Chamberlain. He built the house around the old chimney and used old beams on the original foundation. The Dutton family resided here from 1801 until 1974, when Charles Parlee purchased and refurbished the property.

JOHN SHED HOUSE, 217 PINE HILL ROAD, CHELMSFORD CENTER, BUILT PRIOR TO 1800. The house is an example of an early Cape-style home. John Shed, a cooper, bought the house in 1801 from Col. Ebenezer Bridge.

CAPTAIN BILLY FLETCHER/BATES HOUSE, 26 WORTHEN STREET, CHELMSFORD CENTER, c. 1600s. The house was razed in 1914 to be replaced by a more modern one. The fireplace mantel is on display at the Barrett-Byam Homestead.

JAMES MCFARLIN HOMESTEAD, RIVERNECK ROAD, EAST CHELMSFORD. This was the home of Miss Susan McFarlin, longtime teacher and principal, for whom the McFarlin School was named.

ADAMS/RUSSELL HOUSE, 101 MILL ROAD. This house was built c. 1816 by Joseph Adams, a great-great-grandson of Col. Samuel Adams, who built the first sawmill in town in 1656.

COL. SAMSON STODDARD HOUSE, WESTFORD AND ACADEMY STREETS, CHELMSFORD CENTER, 1706. The house was razed to build the Central Baptist Church.

PAUL DUTTON HOUSE, 10 BARTLETT STREET, CHELMSFORD CENTER, C. 1904. This home is now known as the "Pink House" and has recently been purchased by the town for office space.

WINN/EMERSON HOUSE, 6 NORTH ROAD, CHELMSFORD CENTER, C. 1804. William Benjamin Fletcher may have built this house. Later, Deacon Otis Adams, who is believed to have authored the town motto, "Let the Children Guard What the Sires Have Won," owned the property. Miss Harriet B. Rogers of North Billerica established the first school for the deaf here in 1866. This pioneer school taught students to speak and read lips; it was the forerunner of the Clarke School for the Deaf in Northampton, Massachusetts, which opened in 1867.

Perham house, 30 Dalton Road, Chelmsford Center, early 1700s. The house remained in the Perham family until it was sold in 1957.

Parlor in the Karl Perham house, 30 Dalton Road, Chelmsford Center. Note the tongs, shovel, bellows, and straight-back chair by the fireplace.

J. Adams Bartlett house, 4 Bartlett Street, Chelmsford Center, c. 1678. The house was originally owned by the second minister in town, the Reverend Thomas Clarke, who may have built it. Attorney Oliver Fletcher occupied the house until 1771. Joel Adams Bartlett also lived there and donated the adjoining land for Adams Library.

CAPTAIN JOSIAH FLETCHER HOUSE, 14 CROSBY LANE, CHELMSFORD CENTER, C. 1790.
Captain Fletcher was a private in the Revolutionary War and went to Concord on April 19, 1775, at age 18. He built this house and lived here the rest of his life.

SIMEON SPAULDING HOUSE, 75 NORTH ROAD, CHELMSFORD CENTER, C. 1728.
Col. Simeon Spaulding was a representative to the General Court and was chosen to represent the town in the Provincial Congress. His granddaughter married Dr. John C. Dalton, and they lived here. Dalton Road was named for the doctor. During the 1800s the house was used as a "syndicate" farm, where telephone employees could rest and relax.

ALFRED P. SAWYER HOUSE, BARTLETT STREET AT HIGH STREET, CHELMSFORD CENTER, C. 1903.
After Mr. Sawyer's death, his wife and daughter lived here from 1936 to 1942. The house is decorated here for the town's 250th anniversary celebration.

Bartlett Windmill, 15 Bartlett Street, Chelmsford Center. The windmill was located on the hill behind the Charles Bartlett house and supplied that household with water.

Dr. John C. Bartlett house, 15 Bartlett Street, Chelmsford Center, c. 1698. Dr. Ichabod Gibson probably built this house. His son-in-law, Joel Adams, was a lawyer and began his practice in 1808. Another son-in-law, Dr. John C. Bartlett, began his 46-year practice of medicine in 1831 and had his office in the south side of the house.

RICHARDSON/DAVIS HOUSE, 1 NORTH ROAD, CHELMSFORD CENTER, C. 1840. Samuel Pitts owned this property and sold it to Stephen Pierce, who opened a blacksmith shop in the rear. Joseph Reed, owner of Reed's Tavern, also owned the house at one time. Mary Elizabeth Richardson bought the house in 1867, and her descendants lived there until early in the 1980s. Pictured here during the town's 250th anniversary celebration are, Richard Davis, Mrs. Harold Davis, Miss Jennie Long, Mrs. Nellie Richardson Davis, and Miss Celia Richardson.

MANNING HOUSE, 110 BILLERICA ROAD, CHELMSFORD CENTER, 1816. The house was built by Jonathan Manning in 1816 and was used as a tavern. The opening of the railroad in 1835 took away the tavern business, and it closed in 1838. The property was bought by the town in 1872 and became the Town Farm.

Dr. Francis Kittredge/Howard house, 21 Chelmsford Street, Chelmsford Center, c. 1840. The Greek Revival-style house was built by Dr. Francis Kittredge, whose father lived across the street. Dr. Levi Howard bought it in 1848 and his son, Dr. Amasa Howard, procured it from him in 1895. Dr. Leonard Dursthoff acquired the house in 1924, followed by Henry Eriksen in the 1950s. It is now Dr. Michael Sargent's dental office complex.

Dr. Paul Kittredge house, 20 Chelmsford Street, Chelmsford Center, c. 1831. Dr. Kittredge came to Chelmsford from Littleton, Massachusetts, in 1831. He built this residence and had 14 children, four of whom became doctors. Adams Emerson, an officer in the Civil War, later lived there, followed by Town Treasurer Ervin Sweetser. It is presently a real estate office.

NOON HOUSE, 39 CHELMSFORD STREET, CHELMSFORD CENTER. The home was razed to be replaced by a CVS store.

DADMUN HOUSE, 6 BOSTON ROAD, CHELMSFORD CENTER. Formerly an ell on the J. Adams Bartlett house, this building was moved in 1846 across Boston Road to its present site. It now houses medical offices.

OLD HOME, 41 BOSTON ROAD, CHELMSFORD CENTER.

EDGAR PARKHURST HOUSE, 44 BOSTON ROAD, CHELMSFORD CENTER. This house was razed to make way for the Coach House Apartments. The Parkhurst family members in the picture are unidentified.

HEZEKIAH PARKHURST HOUSE, 47 BOSTON ROAD, CHELMSFORD CENTER, C. 1698–1700. The house was made from two buildings joined together. The northeast room was once a shoemaker's shop, which Hezekiah Parkhurst purchased from Ebenezer Cowdry in 1847. The south part was built in 1698. Descendants of Herbert Emerson and his wife, Eliza Jane (Parkhurst) Emerson, have lived in the house since 1847. It is now the home of the Donald Fogg family.

PUTNAM HOUSE, 118 BOSTON ROAD, CHELMSFORD CENTER, C. 1766. This house was known as Putnam's Farm for many years and noted for fine cider and vinegar. The home at 122 Boston Road was originally a cider mill, but has been a private home for many years.

COBURN/PARKER HOUSE, 134 BOSTON ROAD, CHELMSFORD CENTER, 1760. Jonathan "Trooper Jock" Parker, a trooper in the Revolutionary War, probably built this brick-end house. A field on the property was said to have been a mustering ground for the troops.

SHEREBIAH SPAULDING HOUSE, 203 BOSTON ROAD, CHELMSFORD CENTER, C. 1700. The property was probably part of the estate of Capt. Samuel Adams. His daughters married the Waldo brothers, who sold 260 acres to Andrew Spaulding. The land was kept in the family until Sanford Hazen bought it in 1861. The Harvey family purchased it from Hazen's son's estate.

FISKE HOUSE, 1 BILLERICA ROAD, CHELMSFORD CENTER, C. 1798. This house was built by Simeon Spaulding Jr., son of Col. Simeon Spaulding. An earlier building on the site was owned by Maj. John Minot and included 4 acres from which the small town park in front of the house was later made.

Six

SCHOOLS AND LIBRARIES

CHELMSFORD SCHOOL TEACHERS. Shown here are, from left to right, Susan Emerson, Alice Wheeler, Frances Clark, and Susan McFarlin.

DISTRICT SCHOOL #5 AT CORNER OF LITTLETON ROAD AND OAK STREET, CHELMSFORD CENTER, 1893. From left to right are as follows: (front row) Thomas Sheehan, unidentified, Francis Sheehan, unidentified, Roy Kittredge, Gertrude ?, William Kittredge, Leroy "Job" Dutton, and School Superintendent Knowlton; (back row) William Whitney, unidentified, Grace Mansfield (teacher), unidentified, and Edmund Whitney.

CENTER GRAMMAR SCHOOL, CHELMSFORD CENTER, 1898. From left to right are as follows: (first row) Dora Byfield, Jessie Chamberlin, Ernest ?, Mary Higgins, John Johnson, Nellie Hills, ? Paul, ? Jones, Esther Hills, and Louise Robbins; (second row) Hosmer Sweetser, Raymond Dutton, Alfred Douglas, Leroy Bliss, John Higgins, Ada Kettlety, Laura Richardson, Royal Dutton, and Katie Paul; (third row) Paul ?, Elizabeth Warren, Abbott Russell, and Charles Douglas; (fourth row) Jessie Atwood, Irene Worthen, Edwin Ericksen, Charles Parkhurst, Jeanette Byfield, unidentified, and Ida Lovering; (fifth row) Edward Russell, Fred Russell, Hazel Knowlton, Roberta Parkhurst, Margaret Knowlton, and Ethel Wright.

CENTER TOWN HALL, GRADUATION DAY, NORTH ROAD, CHELMSFORD CENTER, 1914. The stage was decorated with flowers. Note the beautiful grand piano and chandeliers.

CENTER GRAMMAR SCHOOL, CHELMSFORD CENTER, 1915. From left to right are as follows: (first row) Fred Cole, Charlotte Park, Lillian Genest, and Charlotte Kemp; (second row) Florence Linstad and Henry Gifford; (third row) Mildred Hover, Frances Harrington, Katherine Hall, and Winifred Tucker; (fourth row) Cleo Bowers, Harold Linstad, Margarita Ellis, Ruth Putney, and Kenneth Reid; (fifth row) Isador Karp, Mildred Bean, Margaret Hall, Marion Johnson, and Linwood Farrington; (sixth row) George Brown, Gwendolyn Dunsford, Roy Stavely, Eleanor Warren, John Fay, and Miss Susan McFarlin (teacher); (seventh row) Harold Petrie, Hazel McKinley, Allan Adams, Eleanor Ward, and Theodore Emerson.

CHELMSFORD HIGH SCHOOL, CHELMSFORD CENTER, CLASS OF 1916. From left to right are as follows: (front row) Mary Woodhead, Adella Parkhurst, Dorothy Hall, Glendon Scoboria, Edith Adams, and Dorothy Bunce; (middle row) Dorothy Bean, George Paasche, Harry Parkhurst, Edwin Byam, and Gladys Winning; (back row) Mr. Charles Holbrook (principal) and teachers Miss Currier, Miss Hart, and Miss Freeman.

CENTER GRAMMAR SCHOOL, EIGHTH GRADE CLASS, NORTH ROAD, CHELMSFORD CENTER, 1919. From left to right are as follow: (first row) Lillian Pearson, Florence Olson, Barbara Parkhurst, Wilma Perkins, Margaret Robbins Mills, Esther Perham, Mabel Whitbeek, and Margaret McCoy; (second row) Ruth McMaster, Catherine Neillen, Mary Smith, Eva Allard, Hazel Shinkwin, Marjorie Scoboria, and Helen Lucy Sargent; (third row) Roland Blackadar, Laura Marcotte, Miss Susan McFarlin (teacher), and Robert Bartlett; (fourth row) Harold Dunsford, Symon Byam, James Carr, Milton Rounds, Claude Mulaniff, Charles Sargent, Boyd McCrady, Frederick Dane, Ernest Dickinson, and Marion Johnson.

CENTER GRAMMAR SCHOOL, GRADE EIGHT, 1922. From left to right are as follows: (first row) Burton Stokham, Eddie Demaris, Gretchen Manseau, William Ayotte, Donald Dunsford, and Edwin Lundstrom; (second row) Leona Guptil, Eleanor Parkhurst, Ruth Jefts, Helen Stanley, Rachel Byam, Edna Staveley, Kathleen Greeley, Pamela Johnson, Evelyn Boyd, and Grazia Wright; (third row) Jerry Sheehan, Everett Lyons, Lillian O'Neill, Julia Winning, Dorothy Hastings Jensen, Gladys Kemp, Rebecca Winters, Irene Genest, and Ruth Small; (fourth row) Herbert Derbyshire, Herman Olson, Howard Thayer, unidentified, unidentified, Gerald Ivers, Kenneth Billings, and Roland Heald; (fifth row) Milton Stewart, Eliot Parkhurst, Norman Taisey, unidentified, Miss Susan McFarlin (teacher and principal), Tony Pierro, John Whipple, unidentified, and Burton Gould.

PRINCETON STREET SCHOOL THIRD GRADERS, 1931. (Courtesy of Mary Partridge.)

CHELMSFORD ACADEMY ADVERTISEMENT.

102

CHELMSFORD ACADEMY, ACADEMY STREET, CHELMSFORD CENTER. The academy was established in 1859 to provide better education and higher grade classes. However, the Civil War interrupted the progress of this private school, and it closed in 1862. The building had been erected in 1825 for the Chelmsford Classical School of which Ralph Waldo Emerson was the first instructor.

THE MARKER FOR THE CHELMSFORD SCHOOL FOR THE DEAF ON THE COMMON, CHELMSFORD CENTER. The marker was presented by the Clarke School. Alexander Graham Bell met his wife at the school for the deaf, where she was a student.

BRICK SCHOOLHOUSE, FOREFATHERS BURIAL GROUND, 1802. This school replaced the original 1718 schoolhouse and served District Number 1 for 50 years. Bricks for the walls were manufactured at the brick works on Brick Kiln Road, East Chelmsford. The town hearse was also stored here for many years. The schoolhouse was refurbished for the bicentennial observance and is now open for tours.

DISTRICT SCHOOLHOUSE NUMBER 2 AT LOCKE AND DAVIS ROADS, 1870. One of 12 district schools, property at this location was bought from Asa and Elbridge G. Spaulding in 1875. The town sold the property to Frank J. Garvey in 1927; Edward J. Duffy presently owns it. It is reported that the present house was built about 1928 from the old schoolhouse and that markings from the old desks can be found on the sub-flooring.

THE YELLOW SCHOOLHOUSE, DISTRICT ONE, NORTH ROAD, CHELMSFORD CENTER, 1851. The schoolhouse was enlarged to accommodate all grades and the high school. Miss Susan S. McFarlin was the principal-teacher here until the building was razed in 1926, when the McFarlin School was built on Wilson Street. The Central Fire Station now occupies the site.

PRINCETON STREET SCHOOLS AND TOWN HALL, 35 PRINCETON STREET, NORTH CHELMSFORD. These two schools have been razed, and the North Chelmsford Fire Station occupies the site. The town hall is presently being renovated (1998).

SCHOOLHOUSE NUMBER 7, 142 SCHOOL STREET, WEST CHELMSFORD, 1877. Land was purchased from Isaiah Spaulding for the schoolhouse, which was to cost no more than $1,500. The property was sold to the Savage family in 1899 and has been a private dwelling since.

SECOND SOUTH ROW SCHOOL, MILL ROAD, CHELMSFORD CENTER. This school, which had been utilized for many years, later became the Louise Bishop Senior Center. The First South Row School was located across the street and was razed many years ago.

STEDMAN STREET SCHOOL, WESTLANDS. This building was used as a school for many years before becoming the home of the Westlands Improvement Association. It was later sold to become a private residence.

QUESSY SCHOOL, WEST CHELMSFORD. The school was closed when the new North School opened in 1953. It has since been razed, and a private dwelling occupies the site.

SCHOOL-HOUSE SOUTH CHELMSFORD MASS.

SOUTH CHELMSFORD SCHOOL, PROCTOR ROAD, SOUTH CHELMSFORD. In the 1950s, this school became the home of the Chelmsford Grange, and later the Girl Scout house. It was eventually sold by the town and has since been made into a private residence.

EAST CHELMSFORD SCHOOL, 60 CARLISLE STREET, EAST CHELMSFORD. The building is now the home of the Boy Scouts of America, Lowell Council.

HIGHLAND AVENUE SCHOOL, NORTH CHELMSFORD. The school was closed when the North School was built in 1953.

NORTH SCHOOL, 75 GROTON ROAD, 1953. This school burned, and the Chelmsford Senior Center is now on the site.

HIGH SCHOOL, CHELMSFORD, MASSACHUSETTS 5567

CHELMSFORD HIGH SCHOOL, 50 BILLERICA ROAD, CHELMSFORD CENTER. The building was erected in 1916, followed by the gymnasium addition in 1939. It was used as the high school from 1916 until a new and larger school was constructed on North Road. The building became part of the McFarlin Junior High School. It is now utilized as the Town Offices Building.

SOUTH ROW SCHOOL, 250 BOSTON ROAD, CHELMSFORD CENTER.

THE SENIOR CITIZENS CENTER, 75 GROTON ROAD, NORTH CHELMSFORD. The center was built on the site of the North School, which had burned. An apartment complex for seniors is behind the center.

ADAMS LIBRARY, BOSTON ROAD, CHELMSFORD CENTER, DEDICATED IN 1895. The town has had a library since Rev. Hezekiah Packard organized the Social Library in 1794. Books were stored in various places until the library was built on Boston Road. It is temporarily located at the Town Offices Building gymnasium while construction of an addition is taking place at the Adams Library, Boston Road site.

MacKAY LIBRARY, NEWFIELD STREET, NORTH CHELMSFORD. The North Chelmsford Library Association was organized by citizens in 1872. A building on Gay Street was purchased in 1878 for a library until former Selectman Stewart MacKay willed his home on Newfield Street (1947) to the town, as the Anna C. MacKay Memorial Library. Miss MacKay had been active in school and library affairs. She died in 1925 at the age of 35.

Seven

HOUSES OF WORSHIP
AND CEMETERIES

FIRST PARISH UNITARIAN UNIVERSALIST CHURCH, CHELMSFORD CENTER, BUILT IN 1842. The present building (shown here) is the fourth to stand on this site. The town built the brick basement of the building and used it for town meetings and public gatherings until the town hall was constructed in 1879. The steeple blew down in 1876 and was struck by lightening in 1910 and 1955.

FOREFATHERS' BURIAL GROUND BEHIND THE UNITARIAN UNIVERSALIST CHURCH, CHELMSFORD CENTER. The first stone bearing an inscription is dated 1690. The graves of many of the earliest settlers are here along with 45 Revolutionary War soldiers. In accordance with ancient customs, the bodies in the older part of the cemetery are buried with their faces toward the east, as though looking for the promised coming of Christ.

WEST CHELMSFORD UNITED METHODIST CHURCH, 242 MAIN STREET, 1887. This church burned in 1920; the new building was dedicated in 1922.

ALL SAINTS' EPISCOPAL CHURCH, 10 BILLERICA ROAD, CHELMSFORD CENTER, 1882. A parish, at first called Saint Anne's, was established in 1867. In 1868, property was purchased at the corner of Chelmsford Street and Billerica Road. Services were held in the house on the corner until the present stone church was consecrated in 1882. The church sanctuary has been enlarged, and a parish hall was dedicated in 1952.

INTERIOR OF ALL SAINTS' CHURCH, 1867.

FIRST BAPTIST CHURCH OF CHELMSFORD, ACTON AND MAPLE ROADS, SOUTH CHELMSFORD, 1836. The church was established in 1771. The first church building was brought by oxen in the dead of winter from Westford to a site near Heart Pond Cemetery. The present building was dedicated in 1836.

CENTRAL BAPTIST CHURCH, 9 ACADEMY STREET, CHELMSFORD CENTER, 1868. The church was established in 1847 by a group of 35 persons seeking a place to worship closer to home. The Chelmsford Academy building was utilized until the church was built in 1868.

TRINITY LUTHERAN CHURCH, 170 OLD WESTFORD ROAD, CHELMSFORD CENTER, 1964. The Swedish Evangelical Lutheran Church was established in 1882. A church on Meadowcroft Street, Lowell, was dedicated in 1886. In order for the growing congregation to be accommodated, 16 acres of land were bought in Chelmsford for the present church.

IMMANUEL BAPTIST CHURCH, 301 BOSTON ROAD, CHELMSFORD CENTER, 1984. The church was established in 1896 and was previously located on Blossom Street, Lowell, and Billerica Road, Chelmsford, before moving to this building, which overlooks Mill Pond.

GOSPEL HALL, 55 MISSION ROAD, NORTH CHELMSFORD, C. 1905. The church is now the home of the Massachusetts Baptist Temple.

CONGREGATION SHALOM, RICHARDSON ROAD. The main building was dedicated on September 6, 1974, and an addition was built on December 3, 1995. The expansion allowed members to meet their educational and religious needs.

St. Mary's Church, Corner of North Road and Fletcher Street, Chelmsford Center. Founded as a mission of St. John's Church of North Chelmsford in 1921, services were held in Odd Fellows Hall, Central Square, until the new building was ready in 1931. This building was razed in 1965 to build the present church.

St. Mary's Church, North Road, Chelmsford Center, 1965.

ST. JOHN THE EVANGELIST CHURCH, 115 MIDDLESEX STREET, NORTH CHELMSFORD. The parish was founded in 1893. Two previous church buildings were utilized until this new larger complex was built. It was consecrated on November 13, 1963.

SECOND CONGREGATIONAL CHURCH, 17 PRINCETON STREET. This church burned on January 20, 1893, but was rebuilt and dedicated in 1894.

PARISHIONERS AT THE SITE OF THE CHURCH FIRE.

CONGREGATIONAL CHURCH OF NORTH CHELMSFORD, 15 PRINCETON STREET. This church was dedicated on April 26, 1894.

SAINT VARTANANTZ ARMENIAN CHURCH, 180 OLD WESTFORD CHURCH, CHELMSFORD CENTER, 1978. One of the oldest Armenian parishes in the country, it was established on Lawrence Street, Lowell, in 1916. The church moved to Chelmsford in 1978 to the site of the former Belvidere School.

CENTRAL CONGREGATIONAL CHURCH, NORTH ROAD, CHELMSFORD CENTER. The church was erected in 1884 on land donated by the Winn family. The vestry was added in 1892 and the church enlarged again in 1918. It was razed in 1958 when a new church was built at 1 Worthen Street.

122

CENTRAL CONGREGATIONAL CHURCH, UNITED CHURCH OF CHRIST, 1 WORTHEN STREET, CHELMSFORD CENTER, 1958.

ALL SAINTS (EPISCOPAL) RECTORY. The property on which this building and All Saints' Church now stand was purchased in 1868 from the Reverend and Mrs. Horace W. Morse for church purposes. It had been their home while Mr. Morse served as minister of the Unitarian church from 1860 to 1867. Under the new ownership, two first-floor rooms in the house were made into a chapel—Emmanuel Chapel—which was used until the church was built and consecrated (1882).

UNITARIAN PARSONAGE ON LITTLETON ROAD, CHELMSFORD CENTER. This was the home of several early ministers, including Rev. Thomas Clark, Rev. Samson Stoddard, and Rev. Ebenezer Bridge. It was later known as the "Railroad House."

HART/HEART POND CEMETERY, PARKERVILLE AND GARRISON ROADS, SOUTH CHELMSFORD. Land for this cemetery was given to the town in 1774 by Dr. John Betty. In 1776, the wife and two children of Dr. Jonas Marshall died of smallpox and were the first bodies interred there. (Heart Pond is named for its shape when seen from the air. Both Heart and Hart have been written, but Heart is correct.)

TEMPLE BETH-EL CEMETERY, WAVERLY AVENUE, WESTLANDS. This cemetery originated in 1916 with the B'rith Abraham Lodge of Lowell, a mutual aid society of the Hebrew faith, to provide a suitable burial place for its members.

RIVERSIDE CEMETERY, MIDDLESEX STREET, 1841. The cemetery land was purchased from Benjamin Blood and Samuel F. Wood. It was enlarged in 1890.

West Chelmsford Cemetery, Cemetery Way off of School Street, West Chelmsford. Land for the cemetery was bought from John Farrar.

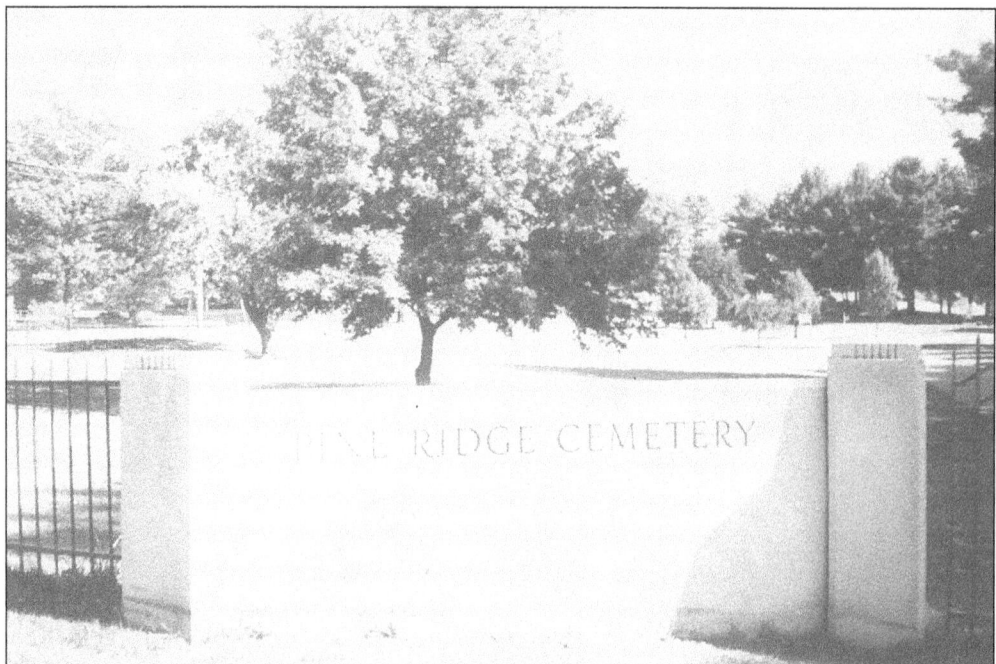

Pine Ridge Cemetery, Riverneck and Billerica Roads, Chelmsford Center, 1888. This cemetery is built on land that was part of the town farm. It has been enlarged several times.

126

St. Joseph's Cemetery, Riverneck Road, East Chelmsford, 1894. The Oblate Fathers, a priestly order of the Roman Catholic Church, were granted this land to be used as the cemetery.

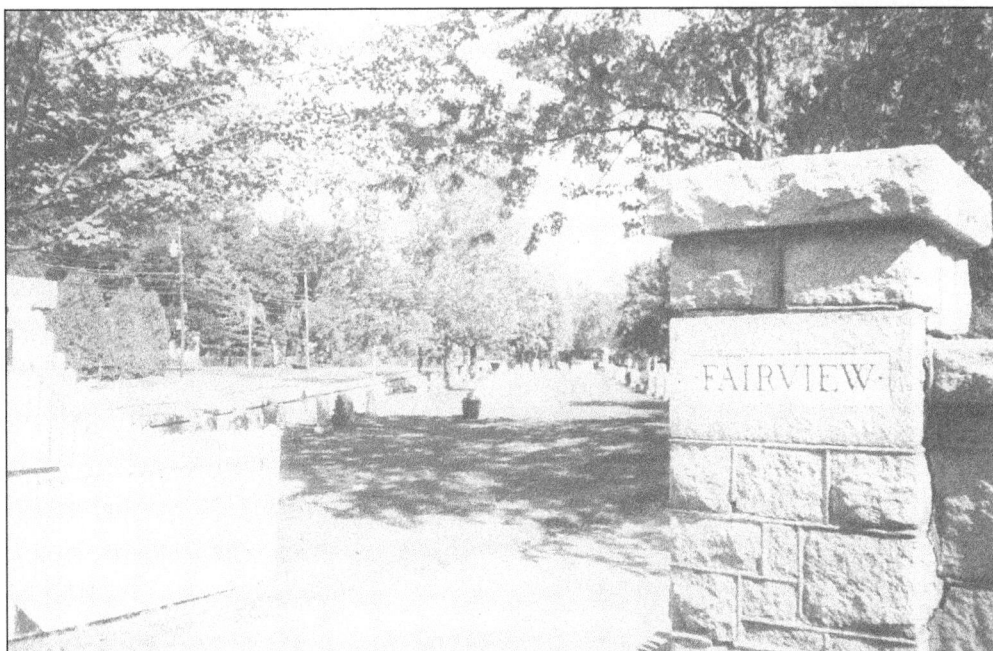

Fairview Cemetery, Main Street at Twiss Road, 1917. Twelve acres of land were purchased from George and Estelle Bowers for this cemetery. The walls and gates were built by the Works Progress Administration.

BIBLIOGRAPHY

Chelmsford Tercentenary Edition: The Chelmsford Newsweekly, 1955.

DeVita, Larose et al. *From Settlement to Suburbia—A New History of Chelmsford*. Chelmsford Public Schools, 1976.

Town of Chelmsford. *Town Report 1977*.

Waters, Wilson, Rev. *History of Chelmsford*. Lowell, Massachusetts: Courier-Citizen Company, 1917.

Wilkes-Allen, Rev. *A History of Chelmsford, New Edition*. Chelmsford, Massachusetts: Chelmsford Revolutionary War Bicentennial Commission, 1974.

www.ingramcontent.com/pod-product-compliance
Lightning Source LLC
Chambersburg PA
CBHW080609110426
42813CB00006B/1456